TREK ON

THE JOURNEY OF A DISCIPLE

TREK ON

THE JOURNEY OF A DISCIPLE

WILLIAM LAMB, Ph.D.

— FOREWORD BY DR. BILLY WILSON —

Director of Publications: David W. Ray
Managing Editor of Publications: Lance Colkmire
Associate Editor: Arleah Waycaster
Layout Design: Shelia Stewart & Stephanie Grable
Cover Design: Jason Williams Creative

ISBN: 978-1-64288-327-5

Please direct inquiries to Pathway Press, 1080 Montgomery Avenue, Cleveland, TN 37311. *www.pathwaypress.org*

The decision to accept Christ as Lord and Savior is made in a single moment, but the follow-through of being a disciple is the journey of a lifetime. *Trek On* by Dr. William Lamb is a book that will encourage and inspire your journey with Christ. Through the lens of his own personal story, along with his unique perspective, you will be challenged to move from a mere transactional relationship with God to a transformational journey of discipleship that will align your path with His path, your plans with His plans, and your future with the future that He desires for you. So, trek on and enjoy the journey!

—Tim Coalter
Presiding Bishop, Church of God of Prophecy

As a marathoner, I was captivated by the author's invitation to run. Dr. William Lamb encourages the reader, through his interactive approach, to join him on a journey for the long haul. It is a lifelong race, a marathon of growing and becoming more like Christ. He challenges fellow runners to trek on in their pursuit of a lifestyle of discipleship. Dr. Lamb has created a tool, a roadmap, a training guide for disciples to run hard and finish strong.

—Gary Lewis
Secretary-General, Church of God

Get ready to be inspired! This book by Dr. William Lamb is a motivational masterpiece on discipleship and leadership. It's packed full of timeless truths and real stories that will push you to become the greatest follower of Christ you can become while challenging you as a leader to not take that journey alone. If you're serious about growing and helping others grow, I highly recommend this book.

—Scott Shepherd
Lead Pastor, Cornerstone Church

Trek On by William Lamb is a compelling and insightful exploration of the eight essential characteristics of a disciple, offering valuable guidance and inspiration for individuals seeking to deepen their spiritual journey. Through engaging storytelling and practical wisdom, Lamb skillfully illuminates the qualities that define a true disciple, providing readers with a roadmap for personal growth and a deeper connection with their faith. By delving into topics such as intimacy, commitment, and integrity, the book offers a thought-provoking perspective on the transformative power of these characteristics in both personal and communal contexts. Whether you are new to the concept of discipleship or a seasoned practitioner, *Trek On* is a must-read for anyone seeking to enrich their spiritual life and embody the virtues of a dedicated disciple.

—Dewayne Moree
Youth Advocate

Through personal stories, Biblical truths and wisdom nuggets, Dr. Lamb provides a much-needed guide to grow as a disciple of Jesus Christ. This book is a great tool for anyone wanting to go "all in" as a *follower* of Christ or be a *leader* for Christ, teaching you practical ways to be a disciple *and* a disciple-maker.

—Sarah Roberts
Fellowship of Christian Athletes, Women in Sports

Dr. Lamb tremendously helped me on my spiritual journey in just over a month. He has provided me with daily devotional books, wisdom, and encouragement, and helped me transition from a non-believer to a Christ follower. He is a great friend who gives support and pushes me to be better daily. His firsthand knowledge of the Lord and His insight has surely changed my life. I trust that the principles in this book will be of help to you as well.

—Malachi Cloud
Student, Lee University

True to form, Dr. William Lamb masterfully weaves practical application and personal experiences into insightful encouragement. For many years, from pulpits to a TEDx Talk, his passionate teachings—fueled by authentic enthusiasm—have had an energizing effect upon disciples of Jesus who desire to become more Christ-like. Now, *Trek On* allows William, like a seasoned coach, to come alongside his readers and offer affirmations, recommendations, and revelations that enhance our journeys and provoke us onward. Anyone aspiring to successfully finish the marathon of life needs this discipleship playbook

—Eric Gilbert
Senior Pastor, 3Trees Church

As someone who studied under Dr. William Lamb's leadership, I can wholeheartedly say *Trek On* is a life guide to being a real disciple of Jesus Christ. The words on these pages take you on a journey to saying yes to the marathon of a life union with Christ. Learn how to trek on and not give up on everything God is calling you to be as His disciple. Enjoy the journey!

—Erica Tuttle
Singer and Songwriter

William Lamb's book *Trek On* dissects the transformative journey from convert to disciple. Through captivating anecdotes and personal experiences, Lamb imparts invaluable wisdom gained from his extensive four decades of ministry. This exceptional book not only inspires but also influences the reader with practical and actionable steps to persevere in the race that lies ahead—like the Apostle Paul's admonition in Hebrews 12:1. Trek on!

—Rob Bailey
International Youth and Discipleship Director, Church of God

I have had the privilege to learn these truths firsthand in class with Dr. Lamb, and I can attest to his passion for discipleship. This book is a great compilation of the wisdom he shares regularly with the people around him. He not only speaks wisdom, but he lives it. In his book *Trek On,* Dr. Lamb gives a practical definition and demonstration of how the life of a true disciple is lived out. Dr. Lamb is highly dedicated to discipleship, and he displays his willingness to teach others the same, inspiring them to be disciples too.

—Emilee Worden
Student, Lee University

Trek On is a must-read for anyone who desires to strengthen their personal and growing relationship as a disciple of Christ. This was one of the most useful and relatable books on discipleship I've ever read. You'll learn not only about the characteristics of a D.I.S.C.I.P.L.E but also the practical ways to apply those characteristics so you can journey on and one day cross the finish line! One word of caution: Be careful when reading. This book could change your life!

—J. C. Worley
Lead Pastor, GO Church

Dr. William Lamb is a tremendous discipler and developer of people. My own children admire his teaching gift, and his practical and powerful style has made an indelible impact on their lives. It is fitting that he writes a book that is so helpful in shaping the hearts of those who follow Jesus. In *Trek On,* he gives a clear blueprint for those desiring to be all Christ has called them to be.

—Kevin Wallace
Pastor, Redemption to the Nations Church

This book is important because of the urgency of its message. With his personal combination of theory and praxis, Dr. Lamb reminds us discipleship is not limited to a class for new believers but a lifelong journey for every Christian. Many new converts make a commitment to follow Jesus but quickly discover that without adequate guidance and accountability, their decision can be short-lived. In *Trek On,* Dr. Lamb moves his readers beyond the haze of understanding and skillfully presents a comprehensive picture of discipleship which can be easily understood by professional clergy and laity alike. He lays out a practical guide to the indispensable pathway of discipleship by outlining eight essential characteristics. As a pastor with a deep concern for the rediscovery of Christian discipleship, this book is a must-read for every believer.

—Dr. R. C. Hugh Nelson
Lead Pastor, Ebenezer Urban Ministry Center

Discovering the infinite nature of God can be challenging. Many times, it's our life experiences and spiritual wounds that try to limit our perception, but when we seek God wholeheartedly, we will always find Him. *Trek On* is a book that shows us how to follow Jesus and to know His voice, no matter the delivery. We live in a time where we must train our ears to hear what the Spirit is saying. This happens through discipline of the Word that shapes us into His faithful disciples. So, prepare for the journey of your life. Get ready . . . set . . . go!

—Amanda Crabb
Pastor, Restoring Hope Church

For the last decade, I've asked my theology students, "What's the greatest challenge facing the church today?" The number one response has been the need for discipleship. Yet sometimes the church has tended to encourage discipleship without giving clear instructions *on how* to become a disciple of Christ. William Lamb's book offers us the *how*! Whether you are an individual wanting to become a faithful disciple or a leader of a group of believers in a church yearning to become more mature in their walk with Christ, both types of readers will experience the joy of learning to be a true disciple. Clearly written and expertly devised to bring practical experience in discipleship of Christ in today's church and world, this book expands Jesus's own command, "Learn of Me."

—Terry L. Cross, Ph.D.
Dean of the School of Theology & Ministry, Lee University

It's common to question the importance of our own lives. *Trek On* serves as a guide for life and gives a unique understanding of the importance of our existence. This book gives us the encouragement and direction we all need. Everyone hopes to make it through life happily; yet, it's impossible to go through life unscathed by hardship. Rarely does a book genuinely point out how to be happy while navigating through hardship the way this book does. I'm grateful to know William Lamb and to learn from him. Do a friend a favor and give them a copy of this book.

—Chris Durso
Author, The Heist: How Grace Robs Us of Our Shame

William offers insightful encouragement in your journey to trek on. If you are starting out or a long-term traveler, this book offers stories of faith and wisdom on staying focused and what truly matters. If you are looking for a spark, a great reminder, or a fresh revelation, this book is for you as you continue to grow in your pursuit of being a disciple.

—Paul Rankin
Chick-fil-A owner/operator (Columbus, Ohio)

ACKNOWLEDGEMENTS
and DEDICATION

This book is a culmination of my life's journey. The stories and personal reflections within these pages provide the reader with an inside view of my life and ministry. This book is also an invitation for you, the reader, to start recording your own stories and shaping your memories into a valuable contribution to others.

While reading, you might think it only takes a few strikes on a keyboard for the author to complete the task. While that might be true for some, it is not the case here. This is work. It is not easy nor is it free. It is work that requires help from others to be successfully completed. It is work that takes endless hours and renditions before public consumption. Even then, I still wonder if the words will connect and inspire the reader. I hope these words will.

It is impossible for me to express my gratitude and appreciation here for everyone worthy of recognition. However, I want to honor a significant few who were instrumental in making this dream a reality. So here is a big shout out to Dewayne Moree, who asked me to write this book; Darren Schalk, my pastor; David Ray and the Pathway publishing team for working with me on a tight schedule; Dr. Michael Reynolds, from the Church of God Division of Education, for placing this book into the required reading sequence. Thanks also to my office team (Heather, Chase, and Valerie) along with student readers (Jocelyn, Grace, Molly, Justin, Lane, Macey, Eli, and Sam); the inaugural board members for Relational Leadership Essentials (RLE), Dr. Johnny Evans and Duane Pace; and the students in my calling and career class at Lee University. I appreciate Jason Williams Creative for the awesome book cover, Dr. Jeff Salyer for always helping me see the possibilities, and Byron Whittington for being a faithful listener and prayer partner. Each of you has contributed to *Trek On*. See you along the journey.

Special thanks for the words written in the foreword from my mentor and spiritual father, Dr. Billy Wilson, president of Oral Roberts University. Billy, you and Lisa have believed in and supported me for over thirty-five years. Don't stop; your voice always matters.

Endless appreciation for my wife, Angela, the most selfless and faithful person I know; for my sons and their brides—Tyler and Megan, Nick and Katelyn, and

Ben and Lexie—for constantly helping me see the value in my work, challenging me never to settle, and to keep doing the good stuff. I pray that someday, my grandchildren (Everlee Grace, Elijah Bennett, Grant William, and the others to come) will be able to understand the principles in this book and become followers of Christ. I pray they carry on the heritage they have been given. I love you all.

Furthermore, I dedicate this book to every disciple of Christ, regardless of your age or experience; to every minister or pastor who reaches out to help others; to every parent and grandparent for loving those entrusted to you; to every high school and college student learning the principles of discipleship and servant-leadership through the RLE brand; to every church leader; every business leader; and every person buying a copy of *Trek On: The Journey of a Disciple.* Never settle. Resist the urge to compromise. Always stay committed to the Gospel.

Greatest praise of all to You, Jesus, for the continued redemptive work You are doing in my heart that makes these stories and principles legitimate. Thank You, Holy Spirit, for the inspiration and energy to write. Thank You, Father God, for calling me to be a disciple of Christ and a preacher of the Gospel; it is the greatest joy of my life.

CONTENTS

FOREWORD

Each year, *Merriam-Webster's Dictionary* selects a *word of the year* based on increased search frequency and substantial use in people's vocabulary. The 2020 word of the year was *pandemic*. In 2021, it was *anti-vaxxer,* and in 2022, the word was *gaslighting.* The word of the year in 2023 was *authentic* as people around the world searched its meaning in terms such as *authentic cuisine, authentic self, authentic voice,* and *authentic faith.*

When I first read that the word *authentic* was gaining such prominence in the English language, I was not surprised. For several years, I have witnessed a growing interest and desire among new generations for the authentic. One of the highest stated values for Generation Z is authenticity. I see this every day in the living laboratory of Oral Roberts University, where I serve as president. This generation wants what is authentic, especially when it comes to their faith. *Merriam-Webster* defines *authentic* as "not false or imitation: real, actual, true; conforming to or based on fact." It can also be defined as "sincere, transparent, and with integrity."

In an age where authenticity is valued, desired, and sought after, *Trek On* is a timely book for this generation. It focuses on becoming an authentic disciple or follower of Jesus Christ. *Trek On* gets beyond the pretense and decorations of Christianity and penetrates the heart of the matter by providing simple, practical steps toward developing our relationship with God. William Lamb encourages our life journey with Christ from chapters on discipline to evangelism. Like a trainer running beside you in a marathon, you will sense that Dr. Lamb understands your journey and has the right words to push you to the next level.

I have known William Lamb for over thirty-five years, and I can attest that he is the "real deal"—an authentic disciple of Jesus Christ. Whether in a college classroom, speaking to a local church or large conference, serving the needy in his hometown, or reaching out to someone in need, William's faith walk is authentic. I have witnessed his dynamic love for people and consistent heart to know Jesus. William is one of my spiritual sons, and I am very proud of his work. He has overcome amazing obstacles in his discipleship journey, from a painful past to a difficult learning disability, so reading his excellent work in this book is a thrill for me. If William can overcome all he has faced to become an authentic Christ follower, then so can you!

The personal anecdotes, Scriptural references, and clear steps forward throughout this book will assist you in your trek on God's path. The road of discipleship is narrow, by God's design. This new and living way is only wide enough for one person at a time, and the door to the path is Jesus Christ himself (Matthew 7:13-14). There are many ups and downs as we follow Jesus; we all have moments when we want to turn back or even give up. Reading and, more importantly, living out the principles outlined in *Trek On* will position you for personal growth and endurance in your walk. In other words, I believe this book will change your life, and I am so glad Dr. Lamb has given us this practical volume to follow.

Enjoy this book and the journey ahead as you trek on. I look forward to seeing you in His presence when our trek is complete.

—Dr. Billy Wilson
President, Oral Roberts University
Chair, Empowered21 and Pentecostal World Fellowship

INTRODUCTION

The year was 1964. The place was Augusta, Georgia. I was a very sick newborn and unexpected to survive, but God had a plan. This was the first verifiable miracle in my life.

The year was 1968. The place was Savannah, Georgia. I lay lifeless on my parents' bed, cool to the touch, both color and breath had departed from my small frame. It seemed hopeless, but my family believed and prayed, and God brought me back to life. This was the second verifiable miracle in my life.

In 1980, I was called to preach, but I had no desire to embrace this burden of ministry. So, after graduating high school, I joined the United States Marine Corps. Then, in 1984, after hearing God speak (audibly) to me, I said yes to my call to ministry. This forever changed my life and the lives of many others.

In 1988, my bride and I verbalized our wedding vows to each other. We are still together today. Over the past thirty-five years, Angela and I have been blessed with three sons, their brides, and three grands. I have since acquired four academic degrees (an A.A., B.A., M.A., and Ph.D., even after failing high school), shared a range of ministry positions and placements, and enjoyed some business ventures along the way. I have preached the Gospel in twenty-five countries and nearly every state in North America. All the while, we are reminded every day that God has a plan.

You might wonder why I shared these dates and snippets of my life. The reason is clear. I wanted you to see the variety of experiences, as well as a glimpse of the complexities that each era of time presented to me. My guess is you also have some dates and times you do and do not cherish. You may have some decisions you need to make about your Christian journey. Perhaps you are already a believer, or maybe you are an unbeliever. Either way, this book is now in your hands. Perhaps you are a lifelong Christ follower able to write the historical account of your faith journey. Regardless of where you are in the process, remember this: God wants you to be close to Him so you have something of value to give others.

Over the span of my ministry, I can account for hundreds, if not thousands, of individuals coming to Christ. The number of disciples I have been able to help develop and cultivate from those numbers is much lower. In full disclosure, those who were or are being discipled by me are only a handful. I do not have a complete account of each one, where they are now, and how their lives have been impacted over time. But they appear in my memory and occasionally on social platforms or in brief personal encounters. I value each one.

A most recent memory of a new disciple of Christ I was able to reach is a student named Malachi. While writing this book, I entered my 21st year in higher education at Lee University. One of the greatest joys over the years has been teaching a class for incoming freshmen called "Gateway." This class includes an introduction to the college experience, a purposeful intent to develop servant-mindedness, and an invitation to pursue a growing relationship with God through an introductory Bible devotion method called S.O.A.P.[1] I usually introduce this method at the beginning of the semester and encourage students to make daily or at least weekly journals of their Bible studies.

In the fall of 2022, Malachi was a quiet but engaged student in my Gateway class. He didn't offer excessive input during the class but would confidently answer if asked. Malachi was a successful high school baseball player and is now a college athlete trying to make it to the big leagues. We connected throughout the semester but never really had a conversation until the last week of class. On that last day, we became connected for the long haul.

At the end of each semester, the students in this class participate in an exit interview. This is a 15-minute conversation about a variety of information pertaining to the class. During Malachi's exit interview, I asked him about his faith journey. At our initial discussion, his faith journey wasn't much to talk about. He did not profess to be a believer or a Christ follower.

At that moment, I felt the presence of the Holy Spirit setting up this conversation. I knew God was working in Malachi's heart. I pulled a small blank notebook out of my credenza, opened it to the first page, and wrote the acronym S.O.A.P vertically. Then, I reminded Malachi of this method of journaling and Bible study. He expressed a lot of interest, and I knew God was doing something significant. I said a prayer for him that day, and we agreed that for accountability, he would text me a green checkmark each time he completed a journal entry. If I were to show you the text exchange between Malachi and me, you would see a long stream of green checkmarks, followed by commentary and even exchanges of Scripture verses.

Just before Thanksgiving break in 2023, Malachi and I met for lunch to catch up. He now has teammates who are accountable to him with their own S.O.A.P. journals and is praying daily for his family and friends to know the Jesus he knows. The big leagues are still in sight, and I promised I would be at his first Major League Baseball game.

The enemy of our souls targets our perception on a regular basis. Is what we see truly as it appears? Are we seeing through the lens of spiritual eyesight or worldly vision? My friend Kevin Wallace states, "Vision is the ability to see the plan and purpose of God for your future."[2]

As you read *Trek On*, **commit** to looking at life through a spiritual lens first. This will enable you to see what others can't see. It will position you to finish strong.

As you read *Trek On*, **pause and reflect** along the way. Reflect on the times God has used you in the lives of others. Reflect on the experiences with other people God has placed in your life. These encounters might seem simple or be marked as miracles.

As you read *Trek On*, **prepare to move** into a stronger relationship with the Creator, which will position you for global impact.

These encounters might be joyful memories or painful reminders. They might inspire you to greatness, not as the world sees greatness, but as God sees greatness.

They might align you with other Kingdom partners. They might just encourage you to keep going. Each encounter has a purpose. So go ahead and learn from each experience. As I tell my students often, "Learn well so you can teach well."

> Whether these encounters are moments or lifelong experiences, each will be a memorable timestamp in your story.

1

TREK ON
The Journey of a Disciple

"I run in the path of your commands,
for you have broadened my under-
standing."—Psalm 119:32 (NIV)

Congratulations! By opening this book, you are beginning the journey of a lifetime. So, let me ask you a question. For some, it will be a no. For others, it will be an automatic yes. But before you answer the question, I want you to take a few minutes to read it out loud repeatedly. Read it five times, pausing and thinking through each question.

Caution! If your eyes automatically went to the questions below and skipped the first paragraph, go back and read the instructions before continuing.

Here we go: read these questions slowly and aloud and think through each before continuing to the next one. Let it sink in. I want you to make an informed decision.

#1 *"Hey, will you join me on a marathon?"*

#2 *"Hey, will you join me on a marathon?"*

#3 *"Hey, will you join me on a marathon?"*

#4 *"Hey, will you join me on a marathon?"*

After reading the question this time, I want you to pause, think about it, and then place a big checkmark in the correct block, reflecting your decision.

#5 *"Hey, will you join me on a marathon?"*

YES ☐   **NO** ☐

Many years ago, I was on the track team in junior high school. Today, it's called middle school. I was in the seventh grade at the time, and because they gave me a team jersey, I thought I was a big deal. Even though I was one of many team members, the track jersey increased my sense of belonging and purpose. In preparation for each season, team members would choose between events like relay races, short and long-distance running, hurdles, sprints, long jump, pole vault, discus throw, shotput, and javelin. I chose to run a short distance even though no one was chasing me. I tried a few other events, but running was my favorite.

While the details continue to dwindle from those days, I will always remember my coach. I never knew his first name because we only called him "Coach Faircloth." Even though he was tough on us, we knew he had a real desire to help. He cared for us. He wanted us to win, so he wouldn't let us be lazy. If we were going to wear the team jersey, we had to commit to work. Faithfulness and loyalty mattered to Coach Faircloth, and we soon learned they also mattered to each of us. Without a commitment to the values of loyalty and faithfulness, we would be dropped from the team.

I only ran track for one year, but it was memorable for me. The value of the team experience, the training that established discipline, the competitive edge, the feeling of victory, and the agony of defeat helped shape me into the man I am today. When speaking of coaches and mentors, be reminded: "Unconditional love doesn't mean a coach isn't demanding or driving or tough; it just means at the end of the day, his or her team knows they are loved."[1]

After that one year of track, I stopped running any type of organized distance until I was a recruit in the United States Marine Corps boot camp stationed at Paris Island, South Carolina. During those thirteen weeks of boot camp, we would run every day. Some days, just a mile or two, but at other times, we would knock out a five-, ten-, or fifteen-mile run/hike.

After boot camp, running was fun again. During my time in the Marines, I ran regularly.

After being discharged from the Marine Corps, running fell off my daily routine until 2012, when I took on another running challenge. One day, I was bragging to my friend Gary Ray about how I was a runner. We decided to run together. I guess I forgot (at that moment) that it had been over twenty-five years since I ran any distance. Be careful what you brag about; you might have to prove it someday. Or, you might be shamed because you can't follow through and end up just a big talker. This was the case with me and Gary. I went out one morning to run a few miles with him, but after half a mile—about a thousand steps—I was weary. We were headed up a hill for about another quarter of a mile, and I was done. I had to walk the rest of the way. I walked while Gary ran up the hill and back down three times, checking on me with each trip. Gary encouraged me to **trek on, not to give up,** and **not to quit.** That day, he taught me another lesson: never leave your friend to run alone.

Never leave your friend to run alone.

Frustrated and embarrassed about my failure to successfully run alongside my friend, I made some serious changes. First, I lost some weight. Second, I became active again every day. After instilling some new disciplines, I gained an interest and even love for running again. A few years later, I became an official marathon runner. Since 2014, I have successfully completed four marathons (26.2 miles) and thirteen half-marathons (13.1 miles).

Many variables affect a person's ability to be a marathoner. These include diet, nutrition, hydration, training, exercise, stamina, weather, terrain, shoes, food and, most importantly, the desire to run. This is the same with life. Many variables affect our day-to-day living. **The most important of all variables is the will to start.** If you said yes to my earlier invitation to run, then pick a race and get started. If you said no, then commit to reconsidering this option later. If your preferred sport is not running, pick something else that is challenging and go for it. You'll be glad you did. The results will be obvious as you develop character, stamina, and endurance.

Calling

You might be wondering what these thoughts on running a marathon have to do with the issue of *calling*. It is simple. Although I was referring to an actual physical marathon where you must run, one foot in front of the other, each of us has a greater race we are called to run. It is a marathon called *life*. It's also about being disciplined to finish well. Discipline has never been an issue for me. I was blessed to have parents and friends to invest in my life and train me well.

When I joined the Marine Corps, I subjected myself to a life of discipline.

But as time progressed, I outgrew the day-to-day responsibility of being disciplined to run since my marine comrades were no longer side-by-side with me. I wasn't in a regiment anymore that mandated my schedule or made me accountable to day-to-day activities, ensuring that I exercised or ran daily. I was on my own, free to do as I wished. While I thought I was free from the expectations of others, I never really was. Neither are you. We are always responsible to someone. Our actions will affect others, always. At this stage in my life, I am accountable to my wife, my children, and my grandchildren, as well as a tribe of other family members, friends, colleagues, and students. You are also accountable to others. You might think your actions only affect you, but that is not the case. Our actions always affect others.

In the space provided, take a few minutes to list the names of people who are impacted by your decisions. This list should matter to you because both good and bad decisions will impact others, and the results of these decisions are often long-lasting.

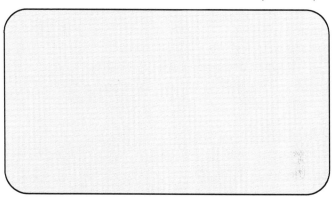

Significance

I still want to invite you to run a marathon with me. It isn't a road or trail race like mentioned before, but rather the marathon of life. At times, it will feel like a long, winding road, with hills and valleys covered with hazards. At other times, you'll be energized by the strength gained by continuing the journey. This journey I speak of is the call to be a disciple. It's a lifelong journey. If you commit and agree to **trek on, to not give up,** and **not to quit,** you *will* cross the finish line.

The Apostle Paul used a running analogy to illustrate the purpose and goal of the spiritual marathon of life:

> Therefore, since we are surrounded by so great a cloud of witnesses, let us also lay aside every weight, and sin which clings so closely, and let us run with

> endurance the race that is set before us, looking to
> Jesus, the founder and perfecter of our faith, who for
> the joy that was set before him endured the cross,
> despising the shame, and is seated at the right hand
> of the throne of God (Hebrews 12:1-2 ESV).

At the finish line of every marathon, the crowds are cheering on the runners regardless of where they are in the pack or what their finish time looks like. I remember from my past marathons that once the end is in sight, the struggle fades away in the sounds of those cheering supporters. We should do the same in the faith journey. Go ahead and cheer somebody on today; it helps.

So, let me ask you one more time. *"Hey, are you ready to join me on a marathon?"* If you are ready, let's go. It is the **most important** marathon of your life. It's an invitation to become a committed follower of Christ and a faithful disciple.

Here's another chance to say yes. Put a checkmark in the box and jump all in.

YES ☐

Two Types of Calling

In Christian circles, churches, institutions, and just plain ordinary places, those of us known as believers have a sense of, or have heard of, the word *calling*. Calling refers to two different schools of thought.

First, when we hear someone talk about their calling, it usually connects with their profession associated with Christianity. This is known as a vocational calling. Typically, this refers to the sense that one is called to preach, teach, sing, do mission work, etc.

Second is the idea that calling pertains to how we live this Christian journey. I refer to this "living out the Christian journey" as the calling to be a disciple. I admit, it sounds less exciting than the idea of being called to do some Christian activity seen on the stage, under the lights, or that we are paid for. But believe me, this call to be a disciple comes first. If we cut corners on this one, the liability is high and costly. Answering the call to discipleship is foundational to one's effectiveness in all areas of ministry—primary or secondary.

Regardless of what we lack or have, God calls each of us to become believers and followers of Jesus Christ. So, do not let anyone or any imaginable demographic keep you from being called to the discipled life. Your future depends on it.

As you read the remaining chapters, consider that as believers, we understand a sense of calling to include being committed to reflecting Jesus, to be salt and light, to run well, and to help others run well; regardless of our profession, our work, or even our play. Answering the inward calling will position us for the outward ministry to others.

We are called **to trek on, to not give up,** and **to not quit.** If you are still reading this book, then I am assuming you said yes to join me on the marathon of life! I am glad you did.

Jesus is counting on you. I believe in you. Let's go!

Looking Ahead

In chapters two through nine, I share stories from my life. First, glean from my experiences as you begin to draft your story of God's goodness and grace. Each of us is on a different level in our faith journey. Some might be ahead of you, and others are perceived to be behind you. Be careful. Do not compare or judge yourself according to others' experiences. Learn from their disciplines and apply them to your life if you want, but do not compare. Comparison leads to judgment. To judge another by what they have or don't have is a dangerous way to live. Choose now to resist the spirit of comparison. To compare can create a false reality that breeds discouragement and defeat, ultimately leading to isolation and loneliness. You were created for community, not isolation. Stay focused on the end goal and keep running—you'll be glad you did.

Second, I am sharing these stories to challenge and inspire you to greatness. Not *greatness* as the world deems it but as Jesus Christ sees it. The world typically defines *greatness* in terms of success, money, status, titles, position and authority, and the accumulation of things—saying you have somehow made it. I am not saying any of these things are wrong in and of themselves. But to be owned or possessed by these things as an indicator of greatness is to miss the mark of genuine greatness.

The heart of this book is to bring the reader into a growing relationship as a disciple of Christ. As described by Dr. David L. Cook, to invite the reader on a journey of greatness known as "selfless exceptionalism."[2]

Once we have received the gift of salvation, we are ready to be discipled in our walk with Christ. Using the word DISCIPLE as an acronym, the following chapters explore spiritual discipline. These eight words are characteristics of a disciple. We'll look at practical ways to apply each characteristic and live effectively in this Christian journey.

First, let's reflect on the words of Jesus to His disciples after His resurrection and just before His return to Heaven. We know this litany of verses as the Great Commission. The command from Jesus to the original disciples was clear. It was invitational. It was personal.

> "All authority has been given to me in Heaven and earth. Go therefore and make disciples of all the nations, baptizing them in the name of the Father and of the Son and of the Holy Spirit, teaching them to observe all things that I have commanded you; and lo, I am with you always, even to the end of the age. Amen" (Matthew 28:18-20 NKJV).

Although this initial command was only to the Eleven,[3] it has echoed into the hearts of every believer for centuries and should be a constant reminder for each of us. Just as Jesus called His followers to leave their daily occupations, families, and towns to follow Him, we are asked to do the same (Matthew 4:18-22). While we may or may not be called to a ministry occupation, **we are all called to a lifestyle of ministry.**

In its simplest form, a disciple is a follower. If you follow another, you could be marked as their disciple. The phrase "make disciples" means to teach and instruct. To be a disciple means to follow precepts and instructions. For Christians, it is more than being a believer; it's a call to follow Christ. Are you willing?

The eight characteristics of a disciple in the following chapters can be achieved when we decide to be obedient. According to the Bible, "To obey is better than sacrifice" (1 Samuel 15:22). Obedience isn't cheap; it will cost you. However, it is the best decision you will ever make. Obedience isn't a destination; it's a lifestyle requiring a lifetime commitment that will pay eternal dividends. Obedience isn't optional for a disciple; it is a way of life. Eugene Peterson defined discipleship as "long obedience in the same direction."

The call to be a disciple is a marathon. If you try to run this race fast and ahead of everyone else, you will ultimately fall. If you run it steady and sure-footed, you will finish well and bring others along on the journey. The table below provides a snapshot of each chapter title and a descriptive term for each characteristic.

In addition, at the conclusion of each chapter, you will find a few questions to reflect on, as well as a QR code that will take you to a webpage for group discussion and more resources.

DISCIPLINE: As disciples, we must choose to be disciplined to prevent being disciplined.

INTIMACY: When I heard God speak audibly to me, I almost wrecked my car.

SEEKING: The good news is God is in plain sight. So, why is it so hard to find Him?

COMMITMENT: Be committed to the commitment.

INTEGRITY: Integrity is easier to keep than recover.

PURITY: Think of purity as a posture instead of a destination.[4]

LOYALTY: Belief always precedes behavior.[5]

EVANGELISM: Some of the greatest evangelists I know have never held an official ministry position and never received a paycheck from a church. They've never taught, preached, or led worship from the stage. They've never traveled abroad or had their names in print.

If you are still reading this book, I am convinced you have embraced this invitation to run a marathon with me—the marathon of life. You are all in. I am happy for you and those who will be impacted by your decision. Look around and invite others to join you.

Trek on, do not give up, and **do not quit.**

I believe in you!

2

DISCIPLINE

"Whoever heeds discipline shows the way to life, but whoever ignores correction leads others astray." —Proverbs 10:17 (NIV)

What is *discipline*? Two schools of thought come to my mind. First, discipline can be a punitive measure (punishment). Second, discipline can be a preventive measure (development). Perhaps you have thought of discipline in these two ways.

When thinking of discipline as punishment, my mind goes to my childhood days, both when I was at school and home. Although I wasn't always guilty of doing wrong, I seemed to always get in trouble at both locations.

I wasn't a bad child, just active—very active. As a young boy, I was thought to have ADHD (Attention Deficit Hyperactivity Disorder) according to my teachers' observations. But in those days, they didn't medically diagnose me accordingly. To deter my active behavior, my teacher(s) wanted to medicate me. My mom wasn't a fan of mood-altering drugs, so she simply said "no." Later in my college years, while studying for the master's degree in teaching, I was officially and accurately diagnosed with the learning challenge known as ADHD. More on that later.

Back to the trouble business. When I would get in trouble in school, that same trouble would be waiting for me at home. This seemed odd because it was happening in an era when computers were mainly for the business world and only acquirable by a select group of consumers, in a world where typewriters were the choice instrument for letter writing, in a world where the telephone still hung securely on the wall or was placed on a tabletop with a long chord covered by a rug to keep us from tripping over it; and in a world where email was as real a possibility as flying cars. I realize for some of you, those examples are prehistoric, but I wondered how information could pass so quickly from school to home since we didn't have the communication tools for everyday life for most everyone now.

Communication from my second-grade homeroom teacher or ninth-grade English teacher was always provided to Lorene (my mom) before I would make it home from school. As a result, discipline was awaiting me at home. Of course, it was the punishment type, not the preventive type. So, without a phone to text or the ability to email, how was my mom always aware of my woes at school? It is called *relationship*. The school leaders knew my mom because she always made it a point to be involved in her children's lives.

Although my mom firmly believed in the corrective measures associated with developmentally based discipline, she also held to punishment-based discipline and correction principles. She believed spanking would help me decide to discontinue mischief to avoid another spanking. Sometimes, it worked, and at other times, it did not. I had my share of spankings and even had some that were supposed to be for my brother because he convinced Mom he was innocent and I was guilty. Lewis and I still might debate that when reminiscing about our childhood days. But I am right!

Through all those days of experiencing punishment-based discipline, one thing was certain—Mom loved us. I knew that because when she had exhausted every other approach to correcting our behavior, moments before she started swinging the switch or hurling that belt, she would say, "This is going to hurt me more than it hurts you." Those eleven words were the biggest lie a parent has ever told a child. It was an odd dynamic.

I see the confusion when looking through the lens of a child. How is it that love causes one to punish another, physically spank another, and bear the burden of correcting a child to prevent a greater failure? But from the lens of a parent, I see the responsibility and burden to correct in love. So, Mom and Dad spanking me did not cause me to doubt their love for me. At times, it made me mad. But when I became a parent, I understood the dilemma of accepting discipline as a positive measure of love, not anger. As one who has experienced and delivered spankings, I can tell you when a loving parent must correct a child, it is painful, but in a different kind of pain. It is heart-wrenching but in a different kind of way. It does hurt. If you are a parent or when you become a parent, you'll understand.

The second type of discipline is preventive—development. Remember the ADHD comments from earlier? Well, it is true. I acquired this condition when I was a child and still have the diagnosis as an adult. For some, it is debilitating, but for me it's a win. Let me explain. If I do not exercise discipline as a preventive (development) measure, then the journey with ADHD will sideline me. There are many days I struggle to focus and prioritize. I am easily distracted or restless, but if I will be disciplined to make the necessary changes needed to overcome my struggles, I win. If I win, everyone around me wins. I believe you can win the battle against any altering condition you face if you exercise the positive and preventive nature of a disciplined life. You may not be free from the memory and limitations associated with your challenges, but you do not have to be sidelined by them. You may require medication at some point, but never use medicine as your "go-to" while ignoring the responsibility to live a disciplined life. The Apostle Paul spoke of this type of discipline:

> Do you not know that in a race all the runners run, but only one receives the prize? So run that you may obtain it. Every athlete exercises self-control in all things. They do it to receive a perishable wreath, but we an imperishable. So I do not run aimlessly; I do not box as one beating the air. But I discipline my body and keep it under control, lest after preaching to others I myself should be disqualified (1 Corinthians 9:24-27 ESV).

The challenge for all of us regarding discipline isn't picking one measure over the other. At times, punishment is necessary for development and maturity. When a child (or adult) disobeys, there will usually be a season of correction, including some actions to prevent the undesirable behavior. Then, at times, we will realize that to obtain the desired outcome or to overcome some undesired outcome, we must exercise discipline as a preventive measure. I call this a disciplined lifestyle.

A disciplined lifestyle requires obedience and sacrifice. **I define *obedience* as "no time lapse between God's invitation to be obedient and our willingness to respond."** An action might not be required immediately, but our willingness to obey is the mark of a disciplined life. Sacrifice is the willingness to resist the invitation of self-indulgence. If one wants to honor God in sacrifice, one must be willing to resist the invitations to self-gratification leading to indulgence. At the end of the day, obedience is better than sacrifice. But I think we can and should exercise obedience and sacrifice in tandem. Willingness to sacrifice is the mark of a disciplined lifestyle.

> *As disciples, we must choose to be disciplined to prevent being disciplined.*

As disciples, we must choose to be disciplined (take preventive measures) to prevent being disciplined (experience punishment). This is not easy in a world with blurred lines of what is right and wrong and professing believers living in the shadows, failing to hold to Biblical, principled lifestyles. One of the most discouraging realities I face is knowing my generation[1] gave space for the younger generations to practice hypocritical living. While this did not begin in my generation, I believe the compromise of believers in one generation introduces the spirit of compromise to believers in the following generation(s). Do not be tricked by the enemy. Stop compromising. Period.

Hypocrisy was prevalent among religious leaders in first-century Israel. Jesus spoke often to this crowd of hypocrites. His messages were clear:

> But woe to you, scribes and Pharisees, hypocrites! . . . Woe to you, scribes and Pharisees, hypocrites! . . . Woe to you, scribes and Pharisees, hypocrites! Woe to you, blind guides. . . . Woe to you, scribes and Pharisees, hypocrites! . . . Woe to you, scribes and Pharisees, hypocrites! . . . Even so you also outwardly appear righteous to men, but inside you are full of hypocrisy and lawlessness. Woe to you, scribes and Pharisees, hypocrites! (Matthew 23:13, 15-16, 23, 25, 27-29 NKJV).

Does this sound redundant? It is. Take time now to pause reading this book and read all of Matthew 23, along with Mark 12 and Luke 20.

After reading those three chapters, confront the compromising spirit that pulls on you and address the propensity to be hypocritical by exercising the necessary disciplines needed to be a disciple.

In what area of your physical life do you need to exercise discipline? In what area of your spiritual life do you need to exercise discipline? In what area of your mind do you need to exercise discipline?

Trek on, do not give up, and **do not quit.**

Disciples have discipline.

3

INTIMACY

"Come near to God and He will come near to you. Wash your hands, you sinners, and purify your hearts, you double-minded."—James 4:8 (NIV)

It seems like it was yesterday, but it happened on September 3, 1984. I was a United States Marine, and this was the day I said "yes." I had grown up in church. My dad was a pastor, so church had been a priority in my life. Even if I didn't like church or wasn't living the Christian life, church was still a priority. Actually, let's call it a requirement. Perhaps this is the same for you. If so, **don't resent it.** Learn from the opportunity to worship together with other believers.

As a teenager living with my parents, I knew going to church would happen every Wednesday night and twice on Sunday. In addition to local, state, and national conferences we attended, a couple of times a year we would have what we called "revival" in our small town. A revival was a gathering of people for a series of church meetings. Often, those revivals would last multiple days and nights, and we'd be at church way past my usual bedtime. It seems there might be another flow of revivals happening today. Embrace them. These moves of God can impact you and others for a lifetime.

In addition to our church services, at least once and sometimes two Saturdays per month, my mom and the other church ladies would meet early in the morning and cook chicken dinners. I never understood why we called them dinners when they were served at lunchtime.

My dad's churches were considered small. So, we depended on the sales from the chicken dinners to help us with the financial responsibility for mission work and other needs associated with bi-vocational ministry. These Saturday chicken dinner days were always fun for me. After snacking in the kitchen, I would jump in the car with my dad to deliver these meals around town. Dad would always have extra dinners on every trip beyond the preordered numbers. At first, I wondered if he was expecting new customers along the way. Occasionally, we'd sell an extra plate or two, but when I learned the real reason for the extras, I was introduced to the heart of God. On every trip, Dad would engage with the neediest among us and share a chicken dinner with them. Dad and Mom believed in providing the same quality to those in need as they did for those who could pay. As a result, my life's mission has been guided by those excursions into the community.

My parents never had much money, but they never lacked life's greatest necessities. These necessities were non tangible but essential to the well-being of their children. These qualities **only come when one chooses to live in an intimate relationship with God.** Mom and Dad always put others first and were thankful, caring, helpful, and self-sacrificing. Their intimate encounters with God shaped their lives into service for God to others.

Intimacy is defined as "closeness." It requires a pursuit. My friend Noah Herrin says, "The best way to cultivate intimacy is through the habit of pursuing it one-on-one."[1]

In relationships, people often think of four types of intimacy: emotional, physical, mental, and spiritual. Here, I am talking about spiritual intimacy or closeness between the great Creator and creation. God wants a relationship with me and you. He wants a closeness with us that causes us to embrace this marathon of life with discipline to always do what is right. This begins with the desire to hear clearly. Are you listening to God? Can you hear Him?

At this stage in my life, I use hearing aids to hear others adequately. While beneficial to everyone else, it can sometimes be frustrating for me. At times, that active (ADHD) side of who I am causes me to play this hard-of-hearing card in my favor. But just as I try to play that card to my gain, acting like I can't hear others, one of my daughters-in-law will quickly call me out for neglecting to wear the hearing aids. The problem isn't wearing or not wearing hearing aids; the problem is the mindset of selective hearing. Even when I am wearing the aids, I can turn the volume up or down. The world is constantly promoting its agenda loudly and accusingly. So, those of us pursuing an intimate relationship with Jesus must choose to listen well. We must turn up our spiritual hearing and tune out the enemy's voice. We must listen intently for the voice of God. And when we hear Him, just say "yes."

My Most Intimate Moment with God

When I heard God speak audibly to me, I almost wrecked my car. It happened on Monday, September 3, 1984, when God spoke along Interstate 81 in Bristol, Virginia.

As a loyal and faithful church member, although I was in the Marines stationed in Washington, DC., I would travel to Cleveland, Tennessee, for our church's annual General Assembly. Plus, it was a time to see Mom and Dad since they traveled from Georgia each year for the same event. When God spoke to me on the long drive from Washington to Cleveland, I thought someone was sitting beside me, although the seat was empty. Immediately, I stopped my car on the side of the road to pause and listen. I was still before the Lord, processing what had just happened. My friend Charlie Weir says, "Stillness before the Lord isn't inactivity; it's anticipation."[2] I was anticipating the next time I would hear God speak to me.

If you were to say, "God spoke to me," I would want to know how He spoke. Did He write you a note on a sticky pad? Did He write His words on the wall or captivate your device screen with His talking head? Did He text you? Did your phone ring with an angelic ringtone you've never heard before? Did lightning flash and thunder roll just before a loud, firm message from Heaven? This sounds crazy. Come on, does God speak audibly to humanity? These questions are real. If I said God regularly speaks audibly to me, some of the people I know would begin to wonder if I was just making it up. I might be tempted to agree with them! I must not use any intimate encounter with God for personal gain or notoriety. So, be confident if He speaks to you. But never market those encounters for public praise or gratification. When God speaks, it is a holy encounter.

Whether you believe me or not, God spoke audibly to me on this single occurrence in 1984. After gathering my bearings as I sat in my car, realizing it was just me there and God was not in the seat beside me, I understood what intimacy was about. It's about a relationship with God so meaningful that when He speaks, we hear Him. It's about accepting God's forgiveness when we deserve judgment. It's about surrendering to His way instead of forcing our way. It's about saying yes.

On that Monday afternoon, God's words to me were clear. He didn't call my name, but He spoke. This wasn't an impression in my mind or heart that made me think I heard Him; I really heard Him. I had never heard Him speak like this before or since. But when God spoke, I heard Him, and I said **"yes."**

Our past is one of the tricks Satan uses to keep us from developing an intimate relationship with God. Of all the people mentioned in the Bible, perhaps David best reflected the closeness with God we can experience and should pursue. David—once a shepherd boy, once a warrior, once a giant slayer, once a king; once an adulterer, once a murderer, but also forgiven; always a worshiper and harpist—yes, that David.

Perhaps someone reading this book feels they are like David. You have experienced the highest of mountains and the lowest of valleys. You, like David, understand the joys of winning and the sorrows of losing. Wherever you are now in this marathon of life, if you need to pause and listen, pull over to the side of the road. Take in the moment and make sure you're listening because God is always speaking in some way.

Herrin continues challenging Christ's followers when he states: "Intimacy with Jesus is a huge part of the church's vocabulary, but is it a part of our daily schedule?"[3] In the words of Pastor Joe Dobbins, "God won't make you follow Him, but He won't stop following you."[4]

Are you pursuing Jesus one-on-one? Are you listening for God's voice? Do you hear Him? What is He saying? How are you responding?

Trek on, do not give up, and **do not quit.**

Disciples value intimacy.

4

SEEKING

"I seek you with all my heart; do not let me stray from your commands."—Psalm 119:8 (NIV)

Have you ever played hide-and-seek, or as some call it, "hide-and-go-seek?" This is a classic children's game in which players hide from the one seeking to find them. They want to be found eventually—but not at first. If I close my eyes and think about it, I can remember times when I was the seeker and a hider. When the person seeking finds someone hiding, the roles are reversed. The person who was found must then seek the others who are hiding. My mind takes me back to my childhood days, even my teen years, and of course, as a dad and a papa, playing this game over and over.

Some people think God plays hide-and-seek with them at times. Nothing could be further from the truth. God isn't hiding from you, me, or anyone else.

God wants to be found by everyone! God wants to be seen in clear view.

I have heard people talk about how difficult it is to see or find God. It reminds me of a church camp where we played hide-and-seek, with the staff hiding first and the students tasked with trying to find us. Because of the staff's experience, we were often able to hide in strategic places, making it difficult to find us. This was because we knew the best places to hide, and the students were often impatient and gave up too quickly.

This camp was surrounded on three sides by a lake, and on one of the sides, it contained a small cliff with about a thirty-foot drop from the land to the water.

Being a Marine veteran, I wasn't afraid of a good challenge. So, one occasion, I slid down the side of the cliff **The good news is, God is in plain sight.** and anchored my feet on a tree limb about 10 feet below ground level and 20 feet above the water. On another occasion, one of my staff peers hid in the rafters at the top of a gazebo. On both occasions, we would have been easily spotted by a student looking over the side of the cliff or looking up into the gazebo. We were both in plain sight, but we were never found in those two hiding places.

The good news is that God is in plain sight. So, why is it so hard to find Him?

While writing the book, I reflected on this chapter with Grace, one of my student interns, who said, "Dr. Lamb, we often make the search for God overly complicated. We try to find Him, or the things that only He can provide, in the strangest places." God is everywhere, but our mindset is such that we don't see Him because we are trained to think He is only in certain spaces. The Old Testament story of the prophet Elijah shows us how this limited thinking can cause us to miss God even when He is right in front of us.

> Then he said, "Go out and stand on the mountain in the Lord's presence." At that moment, the Lord passed by. A great and mighty wind was tearing at the mountains and was shattering cliffs before the Lord, but the Lord was not in the wind. After the wind there was an earthquake, but the Lord was not in the earthquake. After the earthquake there was a fire, but the Lord was not in the fire. And after the fire there was a voice, a soft whisper (1 Kings 19:11-12 CSB).

God wasn't making it hard for Elijah to find Him. God was simply present in a gentle and still, small voice, different from how He had been seen in other occurrences.

God is everywhere, always! You can believe that.

Another reason it can seem difficult to find God is because we limit our perception of who He is or how we should encounter Him—based on our history, upbringing, personal experiences, church or denominational traditions, and even our relational and spiritual wounds. When thinking this way, we not only miss God but also feel we are far from Him simply because He did not respond or show His power in the way we thought He would or should. Do yourself a favor: Try not to limit how you think God should work. Just seek Him, and you will find Him. The Lord said through the prophet Jeremiah, *"And you will seek Me and find Me, when you search for Me with all your heart"* (Jeremiah 29:13 NKJV).

Much of our mental and relational lives are spent in a fast lane amid loud noises and hazardous terrain. This can cause us to default to survival mode. As a result, with limited time schedules and pending deadlines, it is easy to neglect seeking after God because we can't see Him, and we often think He will always be available so we can call out to Him later.

Another danger for us is due to busyness. At times, we can be so busy doing things for God that we do not schedule time to seek Him. Remember the chicken dinner story? While it often seemed like a chore, and

Mom would be covered in flour and exhausted when she finished frying chicken for hours and hours, she never complained. When Dad would spend a couple of hours driving around town delivering those chicken dinners wrapped in Styrofoam containers, the inside of the old Ford LTD would smell like fried chicken. Even when the juice from the green beans or gravy from the mashed potatoes would spill out onto the floor of that old car, my dad never complained. He just kept seeking opportunities to help others.

Mom and Dad were always busy helping others. On every occasion, they would teach their children the value of honoring God by serving others. But, more than that, they taught us personal devotion and seeking God was *always* more important than serving others. It wasn't one or the other. It was seeking God first. Service to others would come out of the abundance and overflow from seeking God first. They taught me that to serve others well, I must first serve God well.

My friend Tim Coalter says, "Jesus calls us into His *presence* before calling us into His *mission*." I agree. When we seek God first, we will be fueled by Him for service to others.

When I lived at home with my parents, this putting God first was noticeable in the mid afternoon and heard in the early morning hours. Dad always prayed out loud, very loud, between 5:00 a.m. and 6:00 a.m. At times, I believed my dad thought God was deaf!

Sometimes, when I would come in from playing outside, Mom would be sitting at the table with her Bible open in study and prayer. This activity was necessary to make a difference in the lives of others; for Mom and Dad, seeking God was always a priority. As a result, I learned this discipline of devotion and prayer. As time progressed, I found myself rising early in the morning to spend time with God. My parents lived this lifestyle before me, which helped shape this discipline in my life. Now, I see this passion in the hearts of my children and continuing even to my grandchildren.

What memories remind you of the value of seeking after God? What disciplines do you need to set in place so you will be consistent in seeking God? Who can you invite to join you in the journey of seeking God daily?

Trek on, do not give up, and do not quit

Disciples seek after God daily.

5
COMMITMENT

"Commit to the Lord whatever you do, and He will establish your plans."—Proverbs 16:3 (NIV)

My wife's name is Angela. We celebrated our thirty-fifth wedding anniversary on July 23, 2023. Thirty-five years is an accomplishment! In some ways, it seems like a lifetime. At other times, it seems like we have just begun this journey. Angela and I both come from families where our parents were married long-term. Angela's mom and dad celebrated their six-tieth wedding anniversary in March 2023, about nine months before her dad's funeral. So, in the context of sixty years, thirty-five isn't very long. I'll take it. Those of you who are married will understand this phrase: Sometimes in marriage, you just have to be committed to the commitment. For those of you who are not married, write it down somewhere.

Be committed to the commitment.

Remember this saying. At some point, in some place in your life, you will have to be committed to the commitment to make it.

Commitment is a choice. It means to be dedicated or to fulfill a promise or agreement. This chapter isn't about marriage. But it is about commitment, and marriage is the singular most consistent activity that is won or lost on the value of commitment. I have often said the only competition in a marriage should be the desire to out-serve the other. There are times when I am sure I have made Angela frustrated or agitated. If truth be told, sometimes I have fun doing things that I know she doesn't necessarily like. Usually, she just smiles and keeps on going. But in those difficult times when it is evident the covenant is strained, when it is easier to be upset than to forgive, we must be reminded that succeeding in marriage and our relationship with God are about being committed to the commitment.

As disciples, we must be committed in every circumstance:

> When tragedy strikes and your family suffers a premature loss, remain committed.
>
> If a tornado hits your house and you must rebuild, remain committed.

If your family is affected by multiple miscarriages, remain committed.

If you lose your job and the future is uncertain, remain committed.

When God seems a million miles away, remain committed.

When you lose friends and family due to the human factor, remain committed.

When disappointment seems to be the norm in your life, remain committed.

If others mistreat you again and again and even again, remain committed.

When today looks like it will be worse than the day before, remain committed.

When it seems everyone else opposes the truth you know, remain committed.

When you are persecuted because of your Biblical beliefs and faith, remain committed.

If you are the only believer in your family, remain committed.

When you have blown it and it seems you can't recover, continue and remain committed.

Each of these scenarios, and countless more, are reminders that being a disciple of Christ is not without pain or loss. Pain and loss are part of everyone's story at some level. How we deal with these realities will usually indicate the level of our faith and relationship with God.

For sixteen years, I served as a volunteer emergency services chaplain. I can't explain to you all the horrible situations I have seen that have negatively impacted others: suicide, murder, car crashes, drownings, fires, and more. As a chaplain, I have been involved with families at their most crucial and critical moments. I have seen parents hold lifeless children, spouses clinging to the deceased body of their mate, and children alive and trapped in a car with their parents who were already dead. The smells and the sounds of these experiences and more, where pain and loss have robbed families, are forever etched into my memory.

When believers face tragedy, they can experience the warmth of a faith community walking alongside them. No, it isn't joyful to experience such pain and loss, but hope in God helps them to believe again. In the middle of the difficulty, their commitment to the commitment provides hope that is not circumstantial.

One experience that reminded me of this kind of strength in faith occurred when I walked with a father behind four caskets at one funeral. This man lost his wife and three children when their minivan collided with a moving train. It's still a graphic memory. As the sun glistened across the four caskets because of the drizzling rain, we walked up that small hill to four open graves in a row. At that moment, I understood what being committed to the commitment means. As this husband and father experienced the most unimaginable loss, he wept but still believed. He believed the Jesus he and his family knew was the same Jesus walking alongside him up that small hill, the same Jesus who went home with him to an empty house, the same Jesus able to keep him over the long haul.

I mentioned at the beginning of this chapter that my father-in-law passed away a few months after his six-tieth wedding anniversary. He died on November 25, 2023, after a long battle with Lewy Bodies Dementia and Parkinson's Disease. On the day of his passing, most of our family was there with my mother-in-law. In my sixteen years in emergency services, I have stood alongside family members in a similar sit-uation hundreds of times. This one was different. I wasn't on a chaplain call. I was a member of the family. The corpse that would soon be rolled out of the house in East Tennessee was a patriarch. He was Wanda's husband, the father of three, and father-in-law of three. The poppy of thirteen grandchildren and five great-grandchildren. A legend. A hero. A faithful follower of Christ. A true disciple.

If time tarries, at some point you will have to say goodbye and pick up the pieces of pain and loss. If time tarries, at some point a member of your family will watch as your corpse is buried, leaving nothing more than your memory.

I pray you will stay committed to the commitment so you can echo what the Apostle Paul said at the end of his life: *"I have fought the good fight, I have finished the race, I have kept the faith"* (2 Timothy 4:7 NKJV).

How are you doing with your commitments? What do you need to do to remain committed to the commitment?

Trek on, do not give up, and **do not quit.**

Disciples are committed to the commitment.

6

INTEGRITY

*"People with integrity walk safely, but those
who follow crooked paths will be exposed."*
—Proverbs 10:9 (NIV)

In his book *Integrity*, Stephen Carter said, "Integrity —all of us are in favor of it, but nobody seems to know how to ensure that we get it. From presidential candidates to crusading journalists to the lords of collegiate sports, everybody promises to deliver integrity, yet all too often, the promises go unfulfilled."[1]

Integrity is defined as being honest. Being honest requires a bit of trust. My mentor and friend Gary Riggins defines *trust* as "a risk survived." I have found this true in so many areas of my life. I add to his definition—that to trust, you must take risks. This makes trust a risky business. In most cases, trust can survive. Unfortunately, there will be moments when trust has been challenged or broken so profoundly that surviving the risk seems nearly impossible.

Because of broken relationships and the human factor (remember, we are all human), sometimes we can trust those we do not know more than those we know. I am not suggesting this is the best pattern, but simply stating the obvious. But trust can be rebuilt.

I have often wondered why this might be true. Perhaps it is because people might feel less judged or condemned by strangers than they do by friends or family. Perhaps this is because the strangers are unaware of our flaws or failures. Or perhaps it is just the mindset of humanity to put on a fake persona when around strangers, although our friends and family really know us—even the good, the bad, and the ugly. I have often wondered why friends and family are less apt to forgive each other than strangers. Perhaps this is because strangers are not experiencing the pain or the memory that is felt by those who know, still feel, and live in the pain of a failure(s). Even if the offended have forgiven the offender, they can still live with the painful memory, making it difficult to trust. That's a lot of "perhaps"!

Perhaps speaks of uncertainty. So, at times we are uncertain why people trust or don't trust. From personal experience and nearly four decades of providing care for many types of people, I know that regardless of the sin committed against you and the pain you have encountered, the healing of mind, heart, and emotions can occur—with God's help. Also, regardless of the sin you have committed against another person and the pain you have caused, the healing of mind, heart, and emotions can occur—with God's help for both of you.

I hope you caught what I just said. Whichever side defines you, the offender or the offended, you can experience the healing of mind, heart, and emotions—with God's help. Pause now and give your brokenness to God; He will help you. If you need to forgive someone, decide now to forgive. If you need to ask someone to forgive you, commit today to find the right time to ask for forgiveness. You'll be glad you did.

Trust is not the theme of this chapter, but it needs to be addressed because trust and integrity are so closely connected. Without trust, it is hard to have integrity. J. R. Fitch explains it this way: "Trust, loyalty, respect: Mess up one, you lose all three."[2]

I once heard the statement that integrity is easier to keep than recover. If you look at individuals who have failed in their integrity, you will see some who have never recovered. You will see some still trying to recover, but it seems they are on an endless cycle of highs and lows. There are others whose failure

Integrity is easier kept than recovered.

was never made public, but the pain holds them in a mental prison. Is it impossible to recover? Not necessarily. But the comeback might take minutes, hours, days, weeks, months, years, or a lifetime. In the mind of some, however, the fallen may never recover.

If you are committed to rebuilding or maintaining your integrity, you can recover—with God's help. He will be with you every step.

Stephen Carter continued to define *integrity* with three required steps. First, we must discern what is right and wrong. Second, we must act on what we have discerned, even at personal cost. Third, we must openly say we are acting on our understanding of right and wrong. For the believer, living out integrity requires praying for discernment, embracing what Scripture teaches as right and wrong, and living out loud.

Discerning Right and Wrong

When a person's integrity is not intact, they will be easily swayed or deceived by untruth. We live in a time when deception is prevalent in most areas of life— fake and real look alike on the surface. We live in a culture where words, principles, and values have been hijacked. To *hijack* means to stop a moving vehicle and steal something. Because of compromise and sin, demonic agendas have hijacked words and symbols and then redefined them from their original meaning to illustrate a preferred meaning. For example, take the rainbow symbol. Originally, the rainbow was a symbol used by God as a reminder that He will keep His promise forever (Genesis 9:12-17). But because of a sinful society, the rainbow symbol is largely associated with the LGBTQ+ movement as a statement of diversity. Be careful what you accept or approve.

Do you see the plan of Satan to distort the things of God? Because of sin, preference, and deception, a symbol created to display God's faithfulness has been distorted to mean something completely different. When I see a rainbow anywhere except painted in the skyline—reflecting its true meaning and the divine artist—I stop to determine if this is a distorted perception or an accurate depiction of the heart of God.

Authentic and genuine disciples of Christ will act on what they know to be true. They will dig into the Scripture and live out the true Biblical meaning. They will stand strong on the Word of God and resist the invitation to compromise. With the guidance of the Holy Spirit, real disciples of Christ will be discerning and act on Biblical truth.

Acting on What Is Right and Resisting What Is Wrong

Acting on Biblical truth will bring God's favor. I pray the words of Luke 2:52 over my family daily: *"And Jesus increased in wisdom and in stature and in favor with God and man"* (ESV).

When I pray this prayer, I ask God to give my family wisdom beyond their years and uncommon favor. Favor that can't be bought, borrowed, manipulated, or bartered. I want my family to have God-sized favor. I want you to have God-sized favor. When I ask for wisdom, I want my family to be wise enough to read the seasons and times of life we are living in. I want the same for you.

We are advised by the Apostle Paul (Romans 13:11-14) to know the times. In the Old Testament, the sons of Issachar *"understood the times"* and were known for having wisdom (1 Chronicles 12:32 NIV).

In a world full of compromise and where carnality is more the norm than the exception, we need to learn to act on what is right and resist what is wrong. To be a person of integrity, you must learn this value of knowing what is right and what is wrong so you can then act accordingly.

Just Say It!

Actions speak louder than words. Perhaps your parents made that statement to you, or perhaps you are a parent who has used those five words to explain to your children the impact of their behavior. The final defining point by Carter suggests people with integrity aren't afraid to speak up and be heard. Satan wants to quiet our voices; this is possible if we struggle to maintain integrity. There have been moments in my life when I realized my actions had made my speaking empty and void. In those moments, I learned that if I live right, the enemy has no ammunition to use against me.

My mother-in-law (Wanda) is a saintly person. She lives what she speaks and speaks according to how she lives. Each Monday night, our family (twenty-five of us now) meet at her house for dinner. At some point in the evening, Memaw will usually read a Scripture verse or a devotion. On a recent night, she talked about the need to be ready for the return of Christ. She warned us to be always aware of our actions and to make certain they are pleasing to God. She challenged us to make sure we are living in such a way that others will see Jesus in us regardless of where we are.

Are you known for having integrity? Are you a reflection or refraction of Christ?

Trek on, do not give up, and do not quit.

Disciples work to keep their integrity.

7

PURITY

I remember the first time I ever saw porn. I was a young teenager, and I immediately closed my eyes. But as soon as I closed them, I remember peeking with one eye shut and the other fully open. At that point in my life, it might have seemed like an innocent action experienced by most teenage boys, but it is no laughing matter. No doubt, many females have also been faced with such a temptation. Porn is not a laughing matter but rather a strong grip that can ruin one's life.

That initial peeking at the page of a naked female body introduced me to the spirit of sexual sin. Thankfully, pornography isn't a temptation for me. It may or may not be for you. Something else might easily trip you up or invite you into darkness. We all have something

Satan places in front of us as a hindrance. Although porn isn't a temptation for me, I realize I am not exempt from Satan's attacks. Neither are you. I learned a long time ago that I have to fight *daily* against darkness and put into place tools to overcome temptation—making it possible to live in freedom. **I want the same for you.** Remember, freedom from addiction doesn't mean freedom from temptation. The enemy will always try to tempt you with something, so avoid temptation as often as you can.

Whatever your struggle is, admit it, confess it to Jesus, repent, and share your struggles with a trusted friend to set up a strong level of accountability. Then, set in place a mechanism to overcome evil before you are overcome by evil.

If I am asking you to be honest, I need to be honest with you. This was the toughest chapter in the book for me to write. The reason is because I realize when one begins to write or talk about purity, Satan desires to remind them of all the times they've failed. So, let me start by saying my list of sins and failures is long. My guess is, so is yours. So, let's make a deal! Be honest with yourself about your propensity to sin and resist the urge to judge others for their sins.

Another reason this chapter was difficult to write is because it required self-disclosure. No, I will not weigh you down with the particulars of my sins. Neither will I ask you to list your own for others to see. However, if you are not dealing with your prodigal pull and sinful actions, others will eventually see and know whatever

Think of purity as a posture instead of a destination.

has a grip on you. When you are set free, stay free. Think of purity as a posture instead of a destination.[1] Purity is a daily commitment. Purity requires action, not just intention. Purity is possible.

Recently, I was immersed in a study of 1 Corinthians when preparing for a class I was scheduled to teach. During my brief refreshing of the book, I was reminded of how corrupt the first-century church of Corinth was. As I continued my cross-reference study, I read multiple occurrences of the sexual perversion that was rampant in the first century, which reminds me of how corrupt our world is now. The Apostle Paul wrote to the Corinthian church:

> I can hardly believe the report about the sexual immorality going on among you—something that even pagans don't do. I am told that a man in your church is living in sin with his stepmother. . . . Don't you realize that those who do wrong will not inherit the Kingdom of God? Don't fool yourselves. Those who indulge in sexual sin, or who worship idols, or commit adultery, or are male prostitutes, or practice

homosexuality, or are thieves, or greedy people, or drunkards, or are abusive, or cheat people—none of these will inherit the Kingdom of God (1 Corinthians 5:1; 6:9-10 NLT).

Other versions include the words *fornicators, sodomites, effeminate, selfish,* and so on. We could add many terms to this list regarding the sins in our culture. The corrupt-mindedness and behaviors taking place among unbelievers today mirror the list of sins in the first century. Sadly, they also mirror the behavior of professing believers. Sometimes, it seems difficult to tell the difference between the actions and behaviors of pagans[2] and believers. This should not be the case. Believers should be different. What one generation permits in excess becomes the common practice of the next.

Because a large portion of the porn industry operates underground, it is difficult to gather an accurate amount of how much money is spent annually. The most recent numbers indicate the lucrative grip of porn was at $97 billion a year in 2016.[3] In 2021, *Economy Watch* reported, according to *toptenreviews. com,* the countries with the largest revenue from the porn industry include China, South Korea, Japan, and the United States.[4]

In my teenage years, it was difficult and even a chore to peek into the darkness without being caught. Now, however, porn is just a click away using a phone or a computer and seemingly secret. This desire for porn is often the result of being bombarded every day by a sexualized society that objectifies women and men for sexual pleasure(s). This appetite for sexual perversion is seen in news reports, movies, music, social media, and typical people showing off their bodies on social network platforms in hopes of being accepted by the world's view of success. If you have been trapped in this mindset as a consumer or contributor, then pause right now. Before reading any further, confess your need for Jesus. Call out to Him. He is waiting. He will help you.

I've included this section on porn as a caution to believers. Be wise. Be different than the world. What might seem innocent will quickly take you down a dark tunnel of addiction, isolating you from others and covering you with a robe of shame. A consistent goal of Satan is to quiet the voice of believers. If he causes us to compromise, this can put us in a cycle of shame and guilt; he has robbed us of our boldness and, ultimately, our voice. Do not let this happen to you. Be honest; it will break the silence. Then, set boundaries and accountability and start walking in freedom.

The Pharisaical Spirit

Avoid the comparison mindset. When we judge another person's sin as more damaging than our own, we begin to fall prey to Satan's attack. You know what this looks like because it is easy to categorize sins—especially the sins of others. In the eyes of God, sin is sin. In the eyes of humanity, some sins are acceptable, while others are detestable. This kind of thinking is a great way to welcome the pharisaical[5] spirit.

Jesus was quick to address this spirit. He called the religious people "vipers" because they were full of greed and self-indulgence while judging others. Once you make room for the pharisaical spirit, that demonic stronghold will take up residence in your mind and actions, ultimately expediting your own demise. **Caution: Never judge others by their actions while judging yourself by your intentions.** Thankfully, God forgives all confessed sins when we repent. However, the consequences of our sinful behavior can trail us for a lifetime.

Sadly, the addictions of believers and non-believers and the strongholds of the world are only going to get worse as time passes. So, prepare yourself for the intense attack of the enemy and remember this: The intensity of temptation or demonic attack seems to increase just before or shortly after a big win. So, keep your guard up.

A Call to Purity

While a lot is mentioned about sexual sins in the Bible, and society tries to woo us with a minute-by-minute invitation to participate in the growing perversion around sexuality, this is not the only area impacted by a call to purity. As a disciple, I want you to pursue a life of purity in body, mind, and spirit.

> Flee also youthful lusts: but follow righteousness, faith, charity, peace, with them that call on the Lord out of a pure heart (2 Timothy 2:22 KJV).

> Finally, brethren, whatsoever things are true, whatsoever things are honest, whatsoever things are just, whatsoever things are pure, whatsoever things are lovely, whatsoever things are of good report; if there be any virtue, and if there be any praise, think on these things (Philippans 4:8 KJV).

The word *pure* means "to be free from carnality; to be chaste, modest, and clean." As Christians, we will differ from non-believers if we're notably free from carnality and living chaste, modest, and clean lives. This decision of purity as a disciple requires us to choose a life of sacrifice over a life of indulgence. *Sacrifice* is the willingness to resist the invitation of self-indulgence.

Recently, while in a church service where addicts came for prayer to be delivered from the grip that sin had on their lives, I witnessed the purest hunger for a genuine encounter with God. Unconcerned with the opinion of the crowd around them, unafraid of possible ridicule, and captivated with the belief that they could be free, I watched people confess and repent of their sins. One individual gave me a glimpse of what desperation looks like. When I asked what she wanted to be freed from, this lady threw her hands in the air as if she was climbing a ladder and yelled, "I want to be free from _____." Her hunger was met with the love of a compassionate heavenly Father who began to pour healing into her body, mind, and spirit, replacing the bondage with liberty.

If you are bound by a spirit of darkness, yell out what you want to be free from, placing your sin in the space: *I want to be free from* _____. If you do so with genuine hunger and desperation, you will be met with the love of a compassionate heavenly Father as He pours healing into your body, mind, and spirit, replacing the bondage with liberty.

Steps to Liberty

Move beyond the mindset of being just a believer to being a Christ follower. For some, it might be a play on words. However, it seems more committed if I implement the belief system I hold dear. For example, to believe Christ is the Savior of the world is a worthy thought, but to follow Christ the Savior requires a commitment. A commitment to be honest with where I am in my journey of faith, to be honest with my struggles and a willingness to resist temptation, to be honest with another about where my weaknesses are before they become my standard practices, and to be sincere with admitting that a life of purity is a daily choice. The way to purity is a commitment to holiness.[6] Holiness brings a promised protection by God. If you walk in relationship with God, pursuing holiness, all of Heaven stands between you and the devourer who seeks to destroy you.

Remember the psalmist David, who we talked about in chapter three? The same guy who was guilty of sexual sin and more? David teaches us how to live a life of holiness, which requires that we pursue God through repentance. He prayed, *"Create in me a clean heart, O God, and renew a right spirit within me. Purge me with hyssop, and I shall be clean; wash me, and I shall be whiter than snow"* (Psalm 51:10, 7 ESV).

Centuries later, the Apostle Peter challenged believers to be holy in our living: *"Since it is written, 'You shall be holy, for I am holy' "* (1 Peter 1:16 ESV).

Purity and holiness are not optional for a disciple. If we are not pursuing a life of holiness and purity, we are not living as Christ's followers. But "as a follower of Jesus you get an advocate on the inside, a voice that is with you, and that voice has a source."[7] For those of us who know this voice, we know all other voices are subject to the Spirit of God. If we are going to win in the battle for good over evil, we must live pure. The Holy Spirit can help us live pure in body, mind, and spirit.

Take time now to pray about that area of your life that reminds you of the guilt and shame you never want to experience again.

What sin are you still trying to hide that you need to deal with? Who do you trust enough to share your secret with so you can shine the light into the darkness of your past and experience freedom?

Trek on, do not give up, and do not quit.

Disciples pursue a life of purity.

8

LOYALTY

"If you love Me, keep My commandments."
—John 14:15 (NKJV)

Are you loyal?

Before you answer this question, let me define the word for you. Being *loyal* means "to give or show firm and constant support to a person or institution." Think about that phrase—*firm and constant support*. To be faithful in allegiance!

At some point in their tour of duty, every marine will serve on a watch known as "guard duty." This requires keeping watch of the area around them. This requires being attentive, awake, and vigilant.

I enjoy military stories and movies. A favorite story is told of the king of Macedonia, Alexander the Great. He was one of the greatest military leaders in the ancient world. It was common for Alexander to eat with his troops, fight alongside them, and walk among them. The story is about a young soldier under Alexander's command who fell asleep while on guard duty. When Alexander heard of this young soldier's failure, he asked, "What is your name?" The boy replied, "Alexander, sir."

The general asked the boy again, "What is your name?"

The young soldier snapped to attention and replied, "My name is Alexander, sir."

Alexander the Great paused, looked deeply into the eyes of the young soldier, and bellowed with a loud and commanding tone, "Young man, either change your name or change your conduct!"

This story reminds me of times I was on guard duty. This responsibility was not for the weak or weary. Regardless of the weather, the circumstances surrounding the post, or any other dynamic, being on guard duty had non-negotiable expectations. We were expected to be attentive, awake, vigilant, and guard our post. We had to fulfill this responsibility with commitment and loyalty. Any act of defiance, cowardly behavior, misconduct, lack of focus, compromise, or any other failure to stand guard would be met with sincere discipline from our marine commanders.

Dr. David Smartt states, "Belief always precedes behavior."[1] Think about that statement. How we believe will eventually be seen in how we behave. You can't separate the two.

I once heard that betrayal trails close behind when a man's loyalty wavers. We can see this as true in the Biblical examples of Simon Peter and Judas Iscariot. Both men were in the original twelve disciples selected by Jesus. Their stories of denial and betrayal of Christ are recorded in the Gospels of Matthew, Mark, and Luke. I am not including the references here because as a true disciple, you will need to dig into the Word of God for yourself. If not now, remind yourself later to read the full account of these two stories. As noted, the Scripture references are not listed here but in the endnotes.[2] This intentionally encourages you to look up the passages, developing your discipline to study.

Belief always precedes behavior.

At the Last Supper, Jesus predicted these two men would fail in their loyalty to Him. Over the next few days, Judas betrayed Christ, and Peter denied knowing Him. Their failures were equally condemning, but Peter repented, while Judas never did. Instead, he ended up taking his own life. I briefly mention these two stories because we must realize that if the twelve disciples were tempted to fail Jesus, we must be assured the enemy of our souls is plotting to trip us up, so we also deny or betray Christ. We must *"be sober, be vigilant because [our] adversary the devil walks about like a roaring lion, seeking whom he may devour"* (1 Peter 5:8 NKJV).

Commitment and loyalty go hand in hand. As you live a committed life, you will build allegiance, and loyalty will result from the commitment.

Now that you more fully understand the meaning, do you consider yourself *loyal*? Are there areas of your life where you have betrayed or denied Christ? If you have been disloyal to Jesus, confess your sin and ask God for forgiveness.

Trek on, do not give up, and **do not quit.**

Disciples are loyal!

9

EVANGELISM

*"He said to them, 'Go into all the world
and preach the Gospel to all creation.'"*
—Mark 16:15 (NIV)

Congratulations! I see you are still with me on the journey of a disciple. I am proud of your commitment to read *Trek On*. Take a couple of minutes now to look at the book cover, which depicts various people groups. All of these people are on a journey. Some started out with others, but as time progressed, they might be trekking alone now. Or, they might have started alone and quickly found community along the way.

I am a runner. At my age, several factors help me select a particular race to run. These include but are not excluded from the cost associated with running, the location, the terrain, and the history or mission of the race. In all the races I have completed, one central theme in choosing that particular race existed:

the number of runners and spectators. While I usually run my own pace and, perceivably, alone during a race, I do not like to run void of people. I want someone else around me from start to finish because I am encouraged by their presence. We are created for community, not isolation. Remember what I wrote about Gary staying with me while I was walking up a long hill? He never left me alone. He ran behind and in front of me but always checked on me. Do the same. Check on others often. Encouragement and accountability are priceless.

My spiritual father, Dr. Billy Wilson, often uses a phrase to remind Christ's followers of our purpose. His words stuck with me from the early years of our friendship, and I now use his words as a reminder in my life. He said, "We must be committed to bankrupting hell and populating Heaven." This is serious business; we can't afford to leave a single person behind.

In case you haven't caught on yet, let me lay out the pattern of the book. If you figured it out, then congratulations! Remember the table in chapter one, with all eight characteristics that describe a disciple? These eight words—*Discipline, Intimacy, Seeking, Commitment, Integrity, Purity, Loyalty,* and *Evangelism*—connect. While each of them can stand alone as an indicator of discipleship, together they send a strong message that speaks clearly to the world about whose we are.

The first seven characteristics are essential to equip us in preparation for the eighth characteristic, which I define as *evangelism*. At the end of each of the first eight chapters, there's a statement beginning with the word *disciples*. For example, "Disciples have discipline," and "Disciples value intimacy."

Using that train of thought, consider this: Disciples create discipline through intimacy and seeking God, which develops a commitment to integrity, purity, and loyalty, **and, as a result, the disciple is better prepared to do evangelism**. The diagram below shows a visual representation of this process.

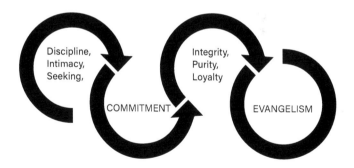

Evangelism is different than discipleship. *Discipleship* is the process of making disciples, which includes helping to produce Christ-like characteristics within others.

Evangelism is spreading the Gospel (the good news of Jesus Christ) in a public or private forum. It can occur through teaching, preaching, or singing, as well as one-on-one dialogue.

In my late teens to mid-thirties, churches were consumed with evangelistic-minded preachers and singers who would share the Gospel from stages and platforms. Today, we still have Christian concerts, conferences, camp meetings, revival nights, and, in some places, longer revivals. In each of these events, lives are being changed and hearts redeemed because of the redemptive work of Jesus Christ through the power of the Holy Spirit. We should celebrate this.

However, there is always a pause in my thinking about these high-octane church events.[1]

Sometimes, I ask myself these questions:

- Is this all there is to the Christian experience?

- Is there more to the Christian way than gathering weekly for a refilling?

- Do people see these events and dismiss Christianity because of hypocrisy?

- Does the world understand what Christians are doing inside the church?

- Does the world want what we Christians have?

- Do these experiences complicate or simplify the sharing of the Gospel?

Please understand what I am saying. I am not speaking negatively of Christian events, churches, singers, and preachers. Even now, we hear reports of new outbreaks of prayer, revival, and renewals. I speak in churches or Christian forums about 70 percent of the year. So, I love these encounters. We need these models of ministry for the cause of evangelism. We need preachers who preach the truth. We need humble musicians and vocalists who lead us into atmospheres of pure worship. We need teachers who educate us on accurate Biblical interpretation and application. We need leaders who will be servant-leaders instead of requiring others to serve them. We need all these people operating in their callings and gifts to build the kingdom of God.

However, the most significant contributions of these ministry professionals will not fill all the needs we have for evangelism. If all the occupational ministry persons were full-time evangelists, we still couldn't reach everyone. To share Jesus with every person on the earth will take more effort and activity than these full-time ministries can offer. It will take everyday people of all ages and vocations who will model the way for others to experience the God of goodness and mercy. Whatever your trade or occupation is, you are called to be a disciple-maker.

In his book *The Power of One,* Dr. Billy Wilson speaks about this:

Everyone needs this message. Yet . . .

- *One preacher can't reach everyone.*

- *One influencer can't reach everyone.*

- *One institution can't reach everyone.*

- *One denomination or movement can't reach everyone.*

- *No group, movement, person, technology, or initiative can reach everyone. Reaching everyone will require everyone.*[2]

Jesus never called us to make converts, but He did call us to make disciples. The conversion business is between deity and humanity, not humanity and humanity. But as Christ's followers, we need to understand each of us is called to evangelize the world.

This word *evangelize* simply means to "preach the Gospel to and to convert to Christianity."[3]

Wait—if this idea of evangelism requires preaching, does everyone have to leave whatever job they are in and sign up to be a preacher? No, not everyone. In some cases, this does happen, and for that, I am thankful. But it is not always a requirement. The Apostle Paul wrote about traditional ministry callings to the church at Ephesus:

> And he gave the apostles, the prophets, the evangelists, the shepherds, and teachers, to equip the saints for the work of the ministry, for building up the body of Christ (Ephesians 4:11-12 ESV).

If you are called to one of these offices in the church, do not look back. Go all in. God will be with you. However, do not limit your thinking that the only way you can make an impact through evangelism is to do so in the frame of traditional occupational callings. Some of the greatest evangelists I know have never held an office, received a paycheck from the ministry, taught or preached from the stage, traveled abroad, or had their names in print. But they are living epistles and image bearers of Jesus Christ.

Some of the greatest evangelists I know have never held an office.

One of my all-time favorite pastors, Dr. Brian Sutton, was noted for saying, "God doesn't need you or me, but He loves us so much that He calls us over to participate in what He's doing."[4] Evangelism is an invitation by God for us to show the love of Christ in and through us as we participate in the most important work of the church. Through a genuine and growing discipleship lifestyle, everything we do should be bathed in a heart for the lost and lived out with a willingness to share Jesus with the world.

Who do you need to share Jesus with today? Go ahead, risk it; they need to know.

Trek on, do not give up, and **do not quit.**

Disciples are committed to evangelism.

CONCLUSION

What's next? Conversion. Building disciplines. Stay committed.

Reaching the multitudes always begins by reaching one.[1] I am one of those "ones" who have been reached and rescued from a life of sin and darkness. Perhaps you are, too. The stories you read in this book are simple reminders of a God of grace and mercy. These stories are excerpts from volumes of memories in my life, both good and bad. Perhaps while reading my stories, you were either reminded or discovered a story about how your life has meaning and value. By default, we often dwell on the bad memories first; but, think of the good memories before revisiting the bad. Living in the positive is always better than dying in the negative. It isn't a play on words but a commitment to discipline our minds to be positive first. If you can't think of any positive memories, let me help you.

YOU matter. The work and play we do is important. It matters. I matter. You matter. We all matter. To *matter* means to be aware of my importance to others and to recognize the importance of others to me. As noted by John Zick in his book *Called*, "Our creative God has uniquely designed every person to fulfill a specific part of His plan."[2] If we fail to fulfill our responsibility in the work that the Creator has designed for us to do, everyone in our circle will be negatively affected by our choice.

Conversion

First, if you are not a believer or a Christ follower, I have been praying for you. If you once were a passionate and committed Christ follower, but now you are cold and indifferent in your faith, I have been praying for you. If you are like Malachi and are ready to know this Jesus you have heard about, I have been praying for you. No, I do not know your name, and we will probably never meet. But I have prayed for the unbelievers, the *backsliders*,[3] and those who are ready to know Jesus. If you fit one of those categories, follow these simple steps to begin or renew your relationship with Jesus Christ.

1. **Admit** you are a sinner who needs a savior. Admit that you need Jesus.

2. **Believe** in your heart that Jesus is the Son of God, and He died on a cross for you.

3. **Confess** that Jesus is Lord. Denounce every other spirit that has held you captive.

If you are ready, take a moment and pray this prayer out loud and let Jesus come into your heart:

Dear Jesus, I admit I am a sinner. I admit I need You in my life. I believe You died on a cross for me, and because of your sacrifice, I can be saved. I confess my sins to you and ask that you forgive me. I confess you are the Lord and make you Lord of my life. Satan is a liar, and I resist him now and forever. According to Zechariah 3:2, I rebuke Satan in Jesus' name. Amen.

If you prayed this prayer of confession and repentance and believed in your heart, then according to Romans 10:13, you have been forgiven and are now saved. Let's go! Welcome to the family of God. It's a BIG family. Let's celebrate. Call someone who needs to know about your new life, and tell them you just gave your heart to Jesus Christ. If you do not have anyone to tell, call me (423-650-6554), and I will celebrate with you and help you find a church where you can grow in your relationship with Jesus and fellowship with others.

Second, as you begin or continue to be a Christ follower and disciple of Jesus, start your own S.O.A.P. journal, beginning with reading the Gospel of John. Here is a starter for you. Stop reading now and take a few minutes to complete the journal entry. Remember, it is personal.

S.O.A.P. JOURNAL

Date:_____ Location:_____

Time: _____ Title: _____

(You can title this entry once it is completed.)

Scripture: *"For God so loved the world, that he gave his only Son, that whoever believes in him should not perish but have eternal life. For God did not send his Son into the world to condemn the world, but in order that the world might be saved through him"* (John 3:16-17 ESV).

Observation: Why were these verses written? What is the main point?

_____

_____

_____

_____

_____

_____

_____

_____

_____

Application: How does this passage speak to you? How can you apply this verse to your life?

_____

_____

_____

_____

_____

_____

_____

_____

_____

Prayer: Write a prayer in response to this passage, and then offer this prayer to God.

_____

_____

_____

_____

_____

_____

_____

Building Disciplines

The second chapter of this book says Disciples *are disciplined*. While there have been plenty of situations over the years where I had to be disciplined because I failed to discipline my own life, I learned the success of my faith journey depends on three non-negotiable principles: *prayer, fasting,* and *daily Bible study*. If, at any point, these principles are not active in my life, I will become stale in my pursuit as a disciple. At that point, the invitation of the enemy to compromise is prevalent, and I can be easily offended, agitated, or self-gratified. This is a dangerous place to be. Guard yourself from this pitfall.

In *The Remnant*,[4] Pastor Larry Stockstill lists what he calls the "Ten Commandments of Ministry." While written with vocational pastors and ministers in mind, these principles apply to all Christ's followers. I suggest you pick up Pastor Larry's book and begin applying these practices in your personal life, which will impact your public ministry. Prayer, fasting, and daily Bible study are addressed by Stockstill's teaching.

Prayer. This seems to be the most unused weapon in the disciple's arsenal. I think this is because prayer seems difficult to wrap our minds around unless we have already developed prayer as a discipline. Jesus said:

> "And when you pray, you shall not be like the hyp-
> ocrites. For they love to pray standing in the syna-
> gogues and on the corners of the streets, that they
> may be seen by men. Assuredly, I say to you, they
> have their reward. But you, when you pray, go into
> your room, and when you have shut the door, pray
> to our Father who is in the secret place; and your
> Father who sees in secret will reward you openly".
> (Matthew 6:5-6 NKJV)

If we pray with improper motives, we have already received our reward. In the original text, the word refers to a receipt signifying "paid in full." The person who prays to be seen or uses prayer for personal advancement will receive human praise and accolades. I would rather have the backing of Heaven than the praise of humanity. I am not saying praise and encouragement are bad. We all need to be encouraged. Just make certain that your motives are not to be seen or praised by people but to be heard by God. Check your motives around prayer and be confident they are pure. If your motives are right, Heaven will respond to the prayers you prayed in secret for all to see: *"Your Father who sees in secret will reward you openly."*

As a Pentecostal, I often participate in the activity of everyone praying together, out loud and sometimes really loud. For the person who doesn't understand this practice of public prayer, it might seem chaotic and too noisy. Don't overthink it. God can hear us individually, even if our prayers are wrapped in a bundle of many other people praying out loud at the same time.

The point is, are we spending enough time in our *closet*[5] praying so we are not a distraction to others when we are praying in public? Ouch—that one makes me think, too. I do not want us to second-guess praying out loud when the opportunity is there or when we feel the urge to do so. I just want our public prayers to be full of power. This can only happen if we have spent appropriate time in personal devoted prayer between us and God. The Apostle Paul taught this principle in First Thessalonians 5:17 when he said, *"Pray without ceasing."* This doesn't mean to pray 24/7 or even constantly. But it does encourage us to be focused on prayer when we are praying and to be faithful in our praying.

Fasting. According to Stockstill, "Prayer is energized by fasting. However, as any spiritual discipline, fasting can become legalistic and unfocused."[6] Keenan Clark said, "While prayer sometimes calls for fasting, fasting always calls for prayer." Fasting without prayer is a diet plan. It seems fasting has often become optional for believers (although it isn't) or limited to a certain time of the year. In the church world, pastors across the globe challenge and encourage their congregations to fast at the beginning of each calendar year. I have participated in these invitations both at individual and corporate levels. The invitation echoes the words of Scripture. Jesus never made fasting optional. In Matthew 6:16, Jesus said *"when you fast,"* not "if" you fast. So, for all Christians, fasting at some level should be a regular discipline. One of the greatest voices regarding fasting, Pastor Jentezen Franklin, models and challenges believers to set aside the first three days of each month to fast. If you have never experienced the value of this discipline, today is a great day to start.

Why should we, or why would we fast? Before answering that question, let's consider good reasons *not* to fast. According to Billy Wilson, we should never fast to (1) obtain merit with God, (2) rid ourselves of sin, (3) lose weight, or (4) be noticed.[7]

Now that we have reasons not to fast, why should we fast? Fasting builds humility. Fasting is about changing us, not God. Fasting opens Heaven's resources. Fasting builds spiritual discipline. Fasting cleanses us from fleshy attitudes and appetites. While fasting does not cleanse us from sin, it does cleanse us from fleshy influences because the discipline of fasting will redirect our hunger toward the spiritual. Fasting can position us to hear the voice of God clearly.

Examples of fasting noted in the Scriptures include the story of Daniel and his three Hebrew comrades (Hananiah, Azariah, and Mishael) in Daniel 1:15-17 and the response from Jesus to His disciples regarding casting out demonic spirits (Matthew 17:14-21). In these passages, we see we cannot do God's work on our own; we need help from Heaven.

For information on Biblical fasting, I suggest you read *Fasting Forward* by Billy Wilson or *Fasting* by Jentezen Franklin. Other Christian leaders also have teachings on fasting that will be helpful. I just know these two leaders model the fasting principle. Of course, you should always consider any medical issues affecting your ability to fast food or water.

Bible Study. While prayer and fasting are vital to being a disciple, daily Bible reading is essential to becoming more like Jesus. We all should desire to be like Him. Being a disciple is not a quick, one-and-done experience. It takes time. We never arrive at being a disciple, but we are always *becoming* a disciple if we are committed to live out the principles outlined here in *Trek On*.

In Ephesians 6:17, the Bible is called *"the sword of the Spirit."* Have you ever played Bible sword drill? For younger readers, let me explain. A leader would call out a Scripture reference in Sunday school or youth group. Whoever found that verse first and read it aloud was the winner. It was a lot of fun. It was assumed the person who won the sword drill knew their Bible better than everyone else. Assumptions are not always reality, however.

As mentioned earlier, the S.O.A.P. journaling method is instrumental in my devotions. I was first introduced to this method by my friend Robert Green, the state director for the Fellowship of Christian Athletes in Tennessee and a veteran youth pastor. Immediately after learning of this approach to Bible study, I applied it and began challenging others along the way. Hopefully, you will try this method, and your family and friends will have volumes of S.O.A.P journals to help cheer them on in this marathon we are all running.

Another essential part of daily Bible reading commitment is understanding the three A's of *hermeneutics* ("the art and skill of correctly interpreting the Bible"). This is a big topic, but here is a brief definition and explanation of the three A's, which can help us accurately interpret what the Bible is saying.

Author. Who is the author? We need to know who wrote the passage we are studying. What is important about the author that impacts how the text was written and how we interpret it? Do not always assume the book's author is the same as the book's name.

Audience. Who is the audience? Who is the author writing to in the text? If we find out who the original audience was, it will help us better understand the message.

Application. How can we apply the principles and teachings evident in the Scripture passage? We must apply the lessons to ourselves before trying to teach or preach them to others. If we let these truths marinate inside us before using them as messages and sermons, your teaching will last.

Remember: Studying the Bible is a journey, not a destination!

Stay Committed

If you are reading these words, you have already expressed an act of discipline and commitment. You are well on your way in this marathon of life. Celebrate it. Go public with your faith and invite others along with you. Staying committed as a disciple of Christ is a daily decision. It is also an individual decision with a communal impact. This decision will have long-lasting effects even after you have passed on to eternity. It is the most important decision of your life.

If you miss a day of prayer,
don't quit. Keep praying.

If you have difficulty fasting,
don't quit. Find what works
and sacrifice your flesh.

If you struggle with daily Bible
study, don't quit. Read a little bit
or a lot, but keep reading.

Final Thoughts

On behalf of your friends and family, I want to thank you for reading this book. They may not yet know the impact of these words on you and them. If you apply these principles to develop the characteristics of a DISCIPLE inside of you, everyone who knows you will soon know.

Trek on, do not give up, and **do not quit.**

I believe in you!

ABOUT THE AUTHOR
William B. Lamb, Ph.D.

Dr. William Lamb is an associate professor of leadership development and the director of the Leonard Center at Lee University (Cleveland, Tennessee). He is a veteran of the United States Marine Corps and volunteered for 16 years as an emergency services chaplain. Lamb holds a B.A. in Religious Studies, an M.A. in Youth and Family Ministry, and a Ph.D. in Organizational Leadership. He served two terms as a member of the Tennessee Governors Commission on Volunteerism and Service.

In his early years between the Marine Corps and joining the Lee University team, Lamb was a school bus driver and business owner in rural Tennessee. His work with need-based students positioned him to impact chaos. His effective and relevant speeches challenge listeners to step into the chaos around them, bringing order and clarity. His storytelling style is applicable across a variety of cultures, organizations, and sectors.

He is easy to understand and knowledgeable in his field of faith, leadership, education, and community.

Dr. Lamb is skilled in helping others look for the not so obvious—a tool for equipping thought leaders to identify deficiencies within organizational systems. Then, he motivates leaders and followers to identify and apply solutions necessary to bring change. He is also a certified facilitator with the Six Types of Working Genius Assessment.

He is an ordained bishop with the Church of God of Prophecy and credentialed chaplain with the Church of God (Cleveland, TN).

For more information on the author or the Relational Leadership Essentials organization visit:

Relationalleadershipessentials.com

You can also reach the site using this QR code:

ENDNOTES

Introduction

1 S.O.A.P is a Bible study method created by Wayne Cordero.

2 Wallace, Kevin. *After This* (Charisma House: Lake Mary, FL, 2021)

Chapter One

1 Cook, David L. *Greatness* (Walsworth: Marceline, MO, 2021).

2 Cook, *Greatness.*

3 Originally, there were twelve disciples, but after Judas betrayed Jesus, there were only eleven.

4 As defined by my student intern, Jocelyn Chavarria.

5 David Smartt (2018).

Chapter Two

1 I was born in 1964 which places me at the end of the baby boomer generation just before the Gen X crowd.

Chapter Three

1 Herrin, Noah. *Holy Habits* (Chosen Books: Minneapolis, MN, 2023).

2 Weir, Charlie. *Hope in Empty Places* (Pathway Press: Cleveland, TN, 2023).

3 Herrin, *Holy Habits.*

4 Joe Dobbins @ Instagram (Dec.18, 2023).

Chapter Six

1 Carter, Steven L. *Integrity* (Basic Books: New York, NY, 1996).

2 J. R. Fitch @Instagram (Dec. 18, 2023).

Chapter Seven

1 As defined by my student intern, Jocelyn Chavarria.

2 *Pagan* is defined by Christians as "one who does not worship God."

3 Newfield, V. & Newfield, A. (2016). United States of America.

4 *https://www.economywatch.com/porn-industry-porn-trade-adult-entertainment-industry,* accessed 10/9/23

5 *Pharisaical* means to be "excessively hypocritical."

6 *Holiness* is defined as "separation from sin."

7 Cook, *Greatness*.

Chapter Eight

1 David Smartt (2018).

2 1 Peter 5:8 (NKJV).

Chapter Nine

1 By *high octane,* I mean church meetings that are high energy or full throttle.

2 Billy Wilson, *The Power of One* (Oral Roberts University Press: Tulsa, OK, 2005).

3 *Merriam-Webster Dictionary.*

4 Brian Sutton, *Prevailing Prayer* (White Wing Publishing House: Cleveland, TN, 2016).

Conclusion

1 Billy Wilson, *The Power of One* (Oral Roberts University Press: Tulsa, OK, 2023).

2 John Zick, *Called* (Pathway Press: Cleveland, TN, 2023).

3 *Backslider* is a term used in Christian circles to describe a person who has lapsed in their previous commitment to Christ, particularly walking away from the life of a disciple

4 Larry Stockstill, *The Remnant* (Charisma House: Lake Mary, FL, 2008)

5 I am not saying to literally go into a closet to pray, although that might not be a bad decision. The point is to find a dedicated place every day where you pray without distractions or interruptions. You can do this. You *must* do this if you want the power of the Holy Spirit in your life.

6 Stockstill, *The Remnant.*

7 Billy Wilson, *Fasting Forward* (Pathway Press: Cleveland, TN, 2005).